Recomn

"Heart, soul, inspiration and tin
words about a vast complexity of emotions. With an empathic
understanding of the creative process, author Warren Sellers mirrors
the mysterious alchemy of songwriting with intuitive prose, deep
compassion and a first-hand knowledge of the enigmatic artistry of
those who can craft an extraordinary song."

Dan Kimpel – Song Biz Editor, Music Connection Magazine

"Little mysteries solved about songs I've always wondered about.
Warren's found a great way to let us in on how these songs came
about…makes me want to listen to them all again…"

Jeff Silbar – Hit songwriter who wrote the Grammy-winning song "Wind
Beneath My Wings" and recorded many other songs including, most recently,
"Wingman" by country star Billy Currington

"Short, easy, informative, with a tug and a tickle. Good bathroom
reading."

Jimbeau Hinson – Singer-songwriter who has written hit country songs such
as "Fancy Free" for the Oak Ridge Boys, "Party Crowd" for David Lee Murphy,
"Hillbilly Highway" for Steve Earle, and many others

"Warren captures the stories of spark and heart behind the songs we
love, and he serves them up as an inspired buffet. Taste and enjoy!"

Scott Krippayne – Singer-songwriter who has written 16 #1 songs for Christian
artists, and other songs recorded by Jordin Sparks, Demi Lovato, Smash Mouth,
Kutless, Kool & The Gang, Paw Patrol Theme (Nickelodeon), also many songs
used in TV placements

"All songs have inspirations, origins, and what I would describe as
the "story behind the song". Warren has found the details and secrets
behind some of the greatest songs ever written and has crafted them
nicely into a story unto itself. I'll listen to those classics with a whole
new appreciation for how they came about!"

Tim James – Hit songwriter who's written two #1 songs (for Toby Keith and
George Straight) and several top ten hits as well

THE JOURNEY OF A SONG

60's & 70's

by Warren Sellers

The Journey of a Song
60's & 70's
Copyright © 2014 by Warren Sellers

Square Tree Publishing
Los Alamitos, California
SquareTreePublishing.com

FIRST EDITION

Cover and Interior Design:
Cathy Arkle - www.cathyarkle.com

To contact the author or for bulk book orders:
info@squaretreepublishing.com

ISBN: 978-0-9903190-0-9

Printed in the United States of America
SquareTreePublishing.com

The Journey of a Song is dedicated to every songwriter who's ever inspired me and to every friend who encouraged me to share these stories.

To my wife, Sherie, thanks for supporting this crazy wonderful journey. To our sons, Josh and Noah, I hope you both find your passions, chase them and surround yourselves with like-minded people. I know I have and do. It's the best gift I ever gave myself.

What's Inside...

60's

70's

Acknowledgements

First to God – The giver of all gifts, for handing me a few gifts I get to run with . . . an awesome creator who loves creation and, thankfully, cares about the desires of my heart. I believe You take joy in my desire to create. I am grateful!

Sherry Ward – Your willingness to do this project alongside me is the key that opened the door. Your generous spirit that wanted to whole-heartedly get involved moves me. Your efforts were tireless, your foresight was right on, your connections were invaluable and most importantly, your vibe was and is good. You got this project from the beginning and connected me to the right folks to put it together. My stories cranked the engine, but you've been driving the dream. You have my endless humility-filled gratitude!

Cathy Arkle – You reached inside my mind and pulled out a picture and a feel and a look that captures this project completely. I wanted it to feel earthy and organic from the front cover to the back and every page in between. You've done that. Thanks for reaching.

Deb Chambers & Susan DeLucca – The editors who read through my pages, did the proverbial "i" dotting and "t" crossing, along with thoughtful unscrambling where needed . . . all while keeping my voice. Thanks for the eyes.

Introduction

Some songs you just come up with...conjure
up a story...manipulate the facts. You
figure it out and fool with it until it all
fits together. It's been done a million
times, done well, and there will be millions
more. But then there are the songs that
were not dreamed up, but rather lived out
and written down by the hands of some of
the greatest songwriters and craftsmen of
all time. Most are real-life stories, or at
least thought-provoking moments, and they
were honest and born from real events.

The Journey of a Song seeks to tell the
stories behind some of the biggest rock and
pop hits of the 60's & 70's, songs that
set the standard for much of the pop-rock
songwriting scene to this day.

My desire is to tell each story as if we are
just hanging out together and I'm simply
talking with interested folks about a shared
love of music and the people that make it.
These are little snapshots of real folks
living "out loud", for generations to come
and for generations to hear.

Hope ya dig...

Warren

60's

It Had to be Hard

It had to be hard, especially from where he was sitting. His name was Jerome Felder.

He had polio as a child and it did a number on his body, so there he sat in his wheelchair at his own wedding watching his wife dance with his brother.

He said it was fine, and he showed his understanding as he hid his discomfort. He learned to live with it, but that memory was a quiet rumbling in his spirit. It all came rushing back three years later when he received an invitation to another wedding. As the feelings resurfaced, he, being a songwriter, did what songwriters do.

He turned over that invitation and wrote out his emotions as he relived that feeling. He wanted to remind the woman in the song to remember who she's going home with at the end of the night, and he simply said...

..."Darling, save the last dance for me."

His name, by then, had been changed to Doc Pomus, a name that sounded more fitting and hip to him in his role as a pop songwriter — and a successful one at that.

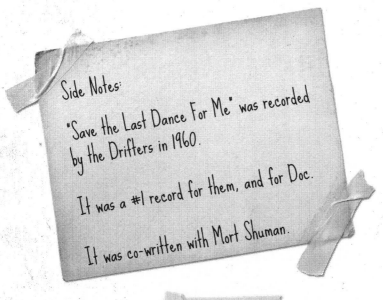

Side Notes:

"Save the Last Dance For Me" was recorded by the Drifters in 1960.

It was a #1 record for them, and for Doc.

It was co-written with Mort Shuman.

The Big Question

It's the age-old question every teenage
girl asks at the edge of her first sexual
experience. After all, there's a lot at
stake...her reputation...her feelings about
herself...her heart...and the really practical
stuff — pregnancy. Well, Carole and Gerry knew
all about that because they had been through
it...the first time...the big question...even
pregnancy. All of those experiences would come
back to serve them in the form of a song.

Carole and Gerry's relationship went beyond
a marriage, into business. They were up-
and-coming songwriters and starting to get
noticed. Carole had written a melody that
she loved and recorded onto a cassette. She
left it for Gerry to listen to that night
when he got home from work. He had a day
job as a chemist and would write at night.
The song, which Carole had already written
the melody for, needed to be a female song
for a group they were hoping to get it to,
called the Shirelles. So, Gerry started
thinking about things from a teenage female
perspective, since he had dated and married
one, and that was the target audience. Love...
relationship...peer pressure...hormones.
That's when he thought about the big question
that surrounds that first night of surrender.
Surrendering to curiosity...to want...to
someone else. So as...

...Carole King's melody played, Gerry Goffin wrote the lyrics to a new song that started with a perfect setup..."tonight the light of love is in your eyes", and then the big question, "but will you love me tomorrow?"

Side Notes:

"Will You Love Me Tomorrow" was recorded by The Shirelles in 1960 and went to #1 on the Billboard Hot 100 chart in 1961.

It has been recorded by other artists such as Brenda Lee, Jackie DeShannon, Cher, Linda Ronstadt, and many more.

My Secret Place

"My Secret Place" — that was its original title, and it was fitting too. When you live in a Brooklyn apartment, the streets are busy, the sidewalks are crowded, and it's hard to find a place to be alone...alone with your thoughts and your ideas, which for a writer is crucial.

Gerry was a writer...a songwriter chasing things to write about. Usually that means writing what you know. Part of what Gerry knew was the big city, bunches of people, the hustle and bustle of it all, and the need for a place to get away from it on occasion. He found one right there in the city. So when the world and the people in it just got to be too much, he'd go up to his secret place, get some perspective, and he'd write whatever he was feeling.

One day, while writing there, he was feeling gratitude for this secret place he had, and it became the center of a lyric of a soon-to-be song...just as soon as he matched it up with the melody-maker in his life, his wife...

...Carole King. His name was Gerry Goffin. He and Carole finished that song, but something about "My Secret Place" just didn't come across as a strong enough title, so the song was written and finished under the name it became famous for, the most obvious choice..."Up on the Roof".

Side Notes:

"Up on the Roof" was recorded by the Drifters in 1962.

It became a big hit in 1963 and went to #5 on the U.S. charts.

"Up on the Roof" has been recorded many times, but the best known is James Taylor's recording of it in 1979. It is still a staple in his repertoire to this day.

Lose the Depth...
Get Me the Dance

That's a loose translation, but it's how Gerry
felt when he wrote it. He preferred to write
songs with at least a little story, a little
something to hang his emotional hat on, but
that wasn't what was needed at this moment.
There are all kinds of ideas that serve as
inspiration — your real life experiences,
someone else's experiences, something funny,
a statement, a picture, a want or a need...
or even a dance. Gerry's publisher, Aldon
Music, was telling all their songwriters that
they needed a smash dance song to rival "The
Twist". "The Twist" was a song and a dance
that was sweeping the country and making
Chubby Checker a household name, so it seemed
like every pop writer was trying to write
their own dance song that would move the minds
and bodies of every teenager out there. But
how do you turn a teenager's attention? After
all, teenage fads were coming and going quick.
You'd have to convince them it's the next
"thing", a "brand new dance that everybody's
doin'", and keep it simple.

Even though Gerry preferred to reach for a
lyric with a little more thought, he realized
kids didn't want to think. They wanted to
dance, so...

...Gerry Goffin, with his constant co-writer, magical-melody-maker and wife, Carole King, wrapped a simple lyric idea into an infectious melody and groove that couldn't be denied. Before long, everybody was indeed singing about a 'brand new dance' as their compelling call went out in 1962 to "come on, come on and do the locomotion"!

Side Notes:

The irony was that there wasn't any dance; the song came first and then they came up with a dance that was described in the song. The dance itself would never be as popular as the twist, but the song was a big hit.

Gerry and Carole had their babysitter, Eva Boyd (nicknamed Little Eva), sing on the recording and released it under the new name of "Little Eva".

"The Locomotion" would go on to reach top 5 status on the pop charts three times in three different decades:
"Little Eva" (#1 in 1962),
Grand Funk Railroad (#1 in 1974), and
Australian artist Kylie Minogue (#3 in 1988).

Homesick

It was 1963, a nasty New York winter to one very cold lady who wasn't used to it because she wasn't from there. Her name was Michelle, and she was there with her new husband chasing musical dreams. The fall in the Northeast is beautiful, but it's also a bit of a warning as to what's coming. But, sometimes dream-chasing means "doing what you gotta do 'til you can do what you wanna do", and in truth they were doing more than chasing their dream. They were actually catching it, but that cold winter had her longing for home.

Her husband, John, was working on song ideas one day and her homesickness served as inspiration. He brought her a verse idea that painted a lyrical picture of winter and all she was feeling, both literally and figuratively, 'cuz the leaves that were beautiful colors a few weeks ago were now just brown, falling to the ground and leaving the trees barren under gray skies. If you're not used to seeing it that barren, the "visual" can just as easily become an emotion that sends your smile into hibernation - just as it was doing to Michelle, by leaving her longing for blue skies and green leaves.

That seed of inspiration grew into a song idea that her husband...

...John Phillips, had. Wishing they were back on the West Coast, or more specifically, dreamin' about California, they wrote the song that was a big part of getting them back there — "California Dreamin'".

Side Notes:

Their group, The Mamas & the Papas (which included Cass Elliot and Denny Doherty), released "California Dreamin'" in September of 1965, but it didn't take off immediately. It wasn't until a radio station in Boston got behind it that it started to fly.

In early 1966, the song went up the charts and landed on #4 and stayed on the charts for 17 weeks.

Many feel the song spoke of bigger picture issues as well, considering the state of things at the time. California represented a lot of the desire for change among music lovers in their teens and twenties in hopes that some of the frozen philosophies of the powers-that-be could find a place to thaw out.

The State of Things

It hung like a cloud in the air, a nuclear cloud, or at least the possibility of it. The world's attention was focused on the gigantic game of chess going on between Russia and the U.S. that only a couple of years earlier had come to a head during the Cuban Missile Crisis. The eyes of the world were watching, and many people were legitimately worried about the possibility of nuclear war; some felt it was imminent.

That was Pete's feeling along with most of his teenage friends in England who were both horrified by it and, strangely, almost resigned to it. Teens who were normally juggling their emotions over finding their place in society now had to wonder about their place in the world, and the possible destruction of it. In some ways, Pete didn't feel like there was much hope for a future, and that it might be horrible anyway. So he wrote about it and poured it into song 'cuz that's what Pete did. He wrote songs for his band, and this was a powerful one, matched only by the power of their singer's voice. You could sure hear the frustration in the vocal, wailing over the never-ending gap between the expectations of society and the distrust they had for those who were running it. That was the backdrop for the song when...

...Pete Townshend wrote about hoping to
die before he gets old. He didn't mean it
literally as much as feeling like it was a
real possibility, given the state of things.
He was really speaking on behalf of, in his
words, "My Generation".

Side Notes:

"My Generation" was written by The Who's
guitarist, Pete Townsend, and released by
The Who in 1965.

It went to #2 on the UK charts and #74 in
the U.S.

It also came out on their album "The Who Sings
My Generation" and on their live album
"Live At Leeds" in 1970.

It Was the Reverb

It was the reverb that took him there...
standing in the bathroom...in the dark. The
natural echo bouncing off the tile makes
everything sound better.

Vibe, it helps you run with your emotion,
opens you up and leaves you comfortably
vulnerable to say the most honest things. In
this case, it sparked an idea, an opening
line to a song filled with the longings of
the early-to-mid-60's and a generation of
teenagers trying to find their way, and their
voice. It was a time of folk music and a
transition to folk-rock music, the music that
spoke to and painted pictures of the state of
things.

In the early 60's, the state of things was
growing increasingly uncomfortable and
chaotic, and it made folks reach for some
comfort, some clarity, some safety and some
quiet — time to think and maybe to write,
maybe even sing...in the bathroom...in the
dark. That's where...

...Paul Simon found himself often, and on one occasion, with all of that teenage angst rolling around his head, it gave birth to an opening line, "hello darkness my old friend...I've come to talk with you again", and the honest musings of a young man absorbing what sometimes only "The Sound of Silence" can bring.

Side Notes:

"The Sound of Silence" was recorded by Simon & Garfunkel and released in 1964. It sold very poorly at first. It was more folk than folk-rock and just didn't fly.

Simon & Garfunkel split up. In June of the following year, producer Tom Wilson over-dubbed electric guitar, bass and drums so that it fit better in the folk-rock landscape, and released it again. Simon & Garfunkel had a hit on their hands and it launched their careers.

In early 1966, "The Sound of Silence" went to #1 on the Billboard Hot 100.

Boss's Orders

Hey, sometimes it's just that simple...the boss calls it out and you need to do it. A lot of times it's not something you look forward to, but there's a job to be done and a deadline to meet. Other times it's not a directive, it's a suggestion — which makes it a whole lot easier. Then sometimes, on a rare occasion, it's a gift in the form of a suggestion to do something you love and would do anyway. This was the latter.

Jerry Wexler, the head of Atlantic Records (the boss), made the suggestion to a very willing-to-hear-it songwriter, Gerry Goffin, and his songwriter-wife Carole King, who together had already written a bunch of pop hits. Carole and Gerry's marriage was in trouble, but their songwriting was in top form. They were about to write one of their last great songs before their divorce, all because of a serendipitous tossing of an idea out of a limousine window. The suggestion from Jerry Wexler, the record label head, was to...

...write a song called "You Make Me Feel Like A Natural Woman". When they showed up at Jerry Wexler's Atlantic Records office a few weeks later with a song called "Natural Woman", two things happened. First, he was surprised they took him so seriously, and second, he loved it. Everybody loved it.

Actually a third thing happened. Aretha Franklin was on Atlantic Records and at the top of her game. It took some doing, but in the end, Aretha Franklin recorded "Natural Woman". It was a big hit and would become synonymous with her.

Side Notes:

"Natural Woman" was released in 1967 and went to #8 on the Billboard chart.

Carole King also recorded it in 1971 on her groundbreaking and standard-setting album "Tapestry".

Pandora's Box

It was 1967. It was the Sunset Strip. The air was thick with philosophical differences between the 'long-haired hippies' and the cops that policed that street. Sunset Blvd was home base for most of the hippies and clubs, such as Whisky a Go Go and Ciros. They, along with the Troubadour (on Santa Monica Blvd), were filled with music that was loved and gathered around. There was another such club called Pandora's Box. It sat on a small concrete island in the middle of the intersection of Sunset and Crescent Heights. At one point, it had a white picket fence that surrounded it and created a small yard that could hold perhaps 50 people. On some nights, there was as many as 200 'long-hairs' that were accidentally causing quite a stir and interrupting traffic. Well, that only sent sparks into the kindling that made up the fragile and contentious relationship between them and the police. So...the city decided to shut it down, and the hippies came out in mass to Pandora's Box to protest that idea. The police took it as a bit of an uprising and treated it like a riot. What it really was depended on who you asked. Everybody had an opinion, including one singer-songwriter who had been making a name for himself. He'd been observing all the related skirmishes and was commenting on the growing issue that was coming to a head. It was a time of uncertainty, fueled by the issues surrounding the Vietnam War, the direction of the country as it related to the war, and the way forward. So, with guitar in hand and those visuals in mind, Stephen Stills began to form a song that became an anthem in a time of uncertainty, with a chorus that called out to both sides. That call was to...

..."Stop and look what's goin' down". The song is called "For What It's Worth" and was the one-and-only big hit for Buffalo Springfield...a band he formed and fronted in 1966, along with Neil Young and Richie Furay. The band took its name from the side of a large piece of equipment used to help refinish asphalt on a street.

Side Notes:

"For What It's Worth" was released as a single in 1967 and peaked at #7 on the Billboard Hot 100 charts.

The song's title appears nowhere in the song lyrics. It came from Stephen playing it for Ahmet Ertegun, the head of their label, and saying, "Here's a new song for what it's worth" - just in passing - and that became the title.

That's the Ticket

That's the ticket that did it. The law's the
law no matter who you are, and he was parked
there too long, so she put a ticket on his
windshield. He came out of the studio where
he was recording and found the ticket and the
parking attendant (known as a traffic warden)
that put it there. This could have been an
irritating moment. The money wasn't going to
be a problem so he asked her name, and when
she told him, it sparked something - but
nothing caught creative fire just yet.

That bit of flame came later when a friend
of his was visiting from America and noticed
a parking attendant, and he said they were
called meter maids in America. That did it...
creative lift off...because meter maid sounded
lyrical to him.

He wondered what a lyric would be like if
someone was trying to get out of a ticket by
flirting with the meter maid instead of being
bothered with the traffic warden. So...

...when Paul McCartney found that ticket on his car outside Abbey Road Studios, it was a magic little moment. It later gave birth to a song about a little run-in with a lovely meter maid who he thought looked like a 'Rita'.

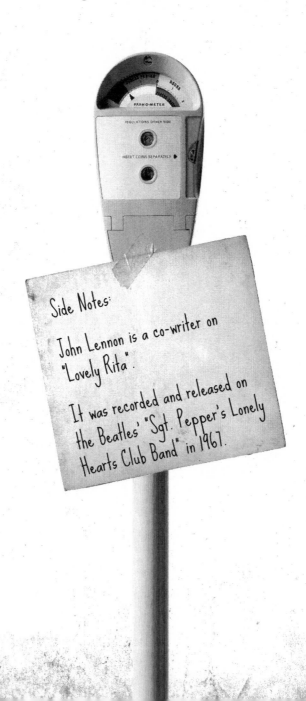

Side Notes:

John Lennon is a co-writer on "Lovely Rita".

It was recorded and released on the Beatles' "Sgt. Pepper's Lonely Hearts Club Band" in 1967.

Jack the Gardener

Jack Dyer was a gardener. He took care of the grounds of a house in the southern England countryside. The owner of the house referred to him as an old English yokel who hadn't been out of the countryside in forever. The English countryside is lush so there was always something to take care of.

Early one very rainy morning, Jack was working on some projects, and because of the rain, he was wearing big rubber boots that made a big sloppy sloshing sound. They got louder and squishier as he went step by step through the mud and the muck.

At one point, he sloshed so noisily past the window of the house that it startled the two men inside who were in a band together and were there writing songs. They'd been up all night and had just fallen asleep when Jack came bouncing by the window. One of them, the singer named Mick, asked his guitar player Keith, who owned the house, who that was, and...

...Keith Richards said to Mick Jagger, "That's Jack. Jumpin' Jack!", and then Mick blurted out, "Flash" - almost as if playing a word association game, and that sealed it. It was beautiful and simple alliteration. It just flowed, and the rest is history. Was "Jumpin' Jack Flash" really a 'gas gas gas'? Apparently! The song sure is.

Side Notes:

"Jumpin' Jack Flash" was released as a single in 1968.

It reached the top of the UK charts and peaked at #3 in America.

Heartache in Four Parts

Heartache. It's nothing new. It's as old as dirt with one constant...ache. It's bone deep and it's all you can think about when you're in the middle of it. You get through it the best way you can. If you're a songwriter, you'll write about it — you have to because the emotions well up until they pour out. Well...Stephen was a songwriter in pain as his relationship was coming to an end. The object of his affection and his ache was Judy, a singer-songwriter making a name for herself. He was crazy about her and those amazing blue eyes. They'd been dating for a while, but the egos and demands of the music biz took their toll, and as they did, Stephen poured his pain out onto paper. He felt he wasn't much fun to be around when everybody was with him all the time.

Four Parts. Maybe it was the back and forth of the emotional dance, maybe the unresolved feelings, or maybe just the brilliance of Stephen Stills — probably a combo. But when Stephen wrote it, he did so in four parts, four distinct musical pieces that all fit in one composition. It's called a...

..."suite" of songs, thus inspiring the title given to his song of heartache over Judy Collins that ultimately became a gift to the world. His heartache, in four parts, is called "Suite: Judy Blue Eyes".

Side Notes:

"Suite: Judy Blue Eyes" appeared on Crosby, Stills & Nash's debut album in 1969.

It was released as a single and went to #21 on Billboard Hot 100.

A Walk in the Garden

Spring had sprung after a typically long English winter, so Eric's friend George came by for a walk in the garden. George was a businessman, but a reluctant one, because he was foremost a musician — a Beatle — and he wasn't enjoying the role of record company executive that he had been thrust into when the Beatles became decision makers at their own Apple label. All the paper signing and shuffling got to be too much, so one day he decided to skip it. The weather was finally decent, so George went over to Eric Clapton's house. He strolled in the garden with an acoustic guitar strapped on, and just sang what he saw and felt...

..."Here comes the sun", and it was more than just alright.

Side Notes:

"Here Comes the Sun" led off side two of the Beatles' "Abbey Road" album in 1969.

She Wasn't Even There

She wasn't even there, but it sure seemed like she was, considering the lyrical picture she painted of the event. She nailed it. I mean she'd heard about it 'cuz it was all over the news. In fact it was the news. The Woodstock Music and Arts Fair took place August 15-17, 1969, and she wanted to be there along with all of her well-known friends. She had become a well-known singer-songwriter herself and was looking forward to it. She and her manager, David Geffen, got as far as New York City, to Geffen's apartment, where the decision was made to stay away because of the perceived chaos of getting in and out of the concert site. She was to appear on the Dick Cavett Show the following Tuesday, August 19, and they didn't want to risk not making it back in time.

So, she watched from a distance as a half million music lovers gathered peacefully and joyfully to celebrate the music they loved, the musicians that performed it, and each other. She felt like she was watching a bit of a modern-day miracle because the media thought it was going to be a nightmare on every level. It looked like it on paper between the rainstorms and the fact that the crowd was so much larger than they were prepared for, but in the big picture, it wasn't. It was common sense defyingly beautiful. It looked like...innocence. She recognized that innocence as a place worth returning to as a society. So, with those images seen on television, along with the eyewitness accounts of her performer friends — including then boyfriend Graham Nash — and without so much as stepping foot in that place she...

...Joni Mitchell, wrote "Woodstock". It turned out to be the quintessential song of the whole event and maybe the whole era. The event was billed as three days of peace and music and that's exactly what it was. In her mind, it was somewhat reminiscent of Eden, and that idea seemed to fuel her lyrical desire to see us all get ourselves "back to the garden".

Side Notes:

Joni Mitchell's recording of "Woodstock" was on her "Ladies of the Canyon" album in 1970.

The most famous recording of the song "Woodstock" was by Crosby, Stills, Nash & Young for their 1970 album "Déjà vu". The album was a huge hit.

It turned out that several performers made it out to join her on the Dick Cavett Show on Tuesday, August 19. It's been referred to as "The Woodstock Show".

The Vase

The vase sat on a shelf in a small antique
store on Ventura Blvd in Studio City,
California. It had been picked up and admired
many times, but that day the hands that held
it belonged to a young artist in a different
medium, a singer-songwriter. Like the match
of a great song with a great singer, this was
a perfect moment between art and art lover.
The young lady who bought it had just finished
breakfast with her boyfriend at Art's Deli
down the street, and as they were walking back
to their car, they stopped into this little
antique store where she found the vase.

The couple then headed up
Laurel Canyon, over Mulholland,
and onto Lookout Mountain, where
they shared a small house that sat
up against a hill.

It was a gray Southern California
morning, cooler than usual, and
that chilly morning turned out
to inspire the good fortune of
millions of music lovers. As
they walked in, he, Graham
Nash, turned to her, Joni
Mitchell, and said...

..."I'll tell you what, I'll light the fire, and you put the flowers in the vase that you bought today". He said 'vase' in his English accent, of course. Then Graham went to the piano, and an hour later, the song "Our House" was complete.

Side Notes:

"Our House" was recorded by Crosby, Stills, Nash & Young on their 1970 album "Déjà vu". It was released as a single that same year and reached #30 on the Billboard charts.

In the late 1960's, Laurel Canyon was home to rock stars and singer-songwriters like Carole King, David Crosby, Chris Hillman, Frank Zappa, Micky Dolenz and many others.

The Irony of the View

Dichotomy, paradox — things that just don't seem to fit. They say opposites attract, and that's true when they compliment each other like puzzle pieces. Other times they repel each other. But even then, if they're forced, they can be made to come together. It was the latter that provoked her pen that day. Her honesty in her lyrics was matched only by her poetry and her innate ability to paint pictures that every willing soul could see.

She was on a trip to Hawaii, looking out the hotel window and taking in the beauty of it all, when she was struck by the conflicted emotion of seeing the growing encroachment of concrete into what looked to her like paradise. It brought a couple different thoughts to her mind about taking things for granted until you don't have them anymore.

It fit her emotion, whether it was a beautiful but disappearing landscape outside her window, dealing with the downside of progress in other areas of life and society, or the loss of a lover. It's all the same emotion, and she said so in a song about the thought-provoking irony of the view outside her window. It was a lyrical lament that became the fuel for...

...Joni Mitchell, when she wrote her song "Big Yellow Taxi", recognizing equal parts for necessity and sadness when trading paradise for parking lots.

Side Notes:

Joni Mitchell recorded "Big Yellow Taxi" in 1970.

It reached #67 in the U.S. in 1970. She later released a live version in 1975 that went to #24.

It has also been recorded by other artists, including Amy Grant and Counting Crows.

Majnun's Girl

Majnun was a character in a Persian love story. In the story, Majnun fell in love with a girl he couldn't have because her father forbade it, and Majnun felt like he was wasting away from unfulfilled desire.

That story was told to Eric Clapton by a friend and it resonated powerfully with him, because Eric was feeling the same about a girl. She was beautiful, interested... but married. She was also lonely because she felt her husband wasn't paying enough attention to her. But Eric was, and she leaned into it. However, Eric did more than lean; he fell hard. Her name was Patty, and the husband who was not paying enough attention was a friend of Eric's. He was George Harrison, the Beatle. These were strange times, often drug and alcohol-fueled, and some heavy things were taken way too lightly. Eric wanted her to leave George and said so in words that finally fell onto paper and across guitar strings. He cried out, "What do you do when you get lonely, and nobody's waiting by your side?" Eric wrote it straight to her and as honest as it gets, except not everyone knew it at first. He didn't use her name — that would have been way too obvious and further complicate an already complicated situation. So, he needed a name that was both relevant and a bit covert, and...

...that's where Majnun's story comes into play...Majnun's girl — the one he couldn't have. Her name was Layla.

Side Notes:

"Layla" was co-written with Jim Gordon and released by Eric's band, Derek and the Dominos, on their album "Layla and Other Assorted Love Songs" in 1970.

Patty Boyd did finally divorce George Harrison in 1974 and married Eric in 1979. George attended the wedding party.

Eric and Patty divorced in 1989.

It Was Billy's Comment

It was quick; it was casual. He said it
repeatedly, it was the sign of the times.
When Billy said it, there were several people
within earshot, but only one really heard it.

Stephen was a songwriter, and songwriters hear
things differently. They hear what is said,
and when it hits them just right, they wonder
what more can be said about it. Sometimes it
depends on who says it — their credibility and
their level of hip.

Well, Billy was hip...serious 'street cred'.
Billy Preston was in the Beatles' camp,
considered the fifth Beatle because he played
keyboards on "The White Album", "Abbey Road",
and "Let It Be". When Billy said it, Stephen —
Stephen Stills — thought it could be the hook
line of a song, and he was right.

At the time, it was about as relevant as
anything could be. What Billy said was...

..."If you can't be with the one you love — love the one you're with".

Side Notes:

It was Stephen Stills' first single off his solo debut album called "Stephen Stills". David Crosby and Graham Nash - among others - sang background vocals.

Released in 1970, "Love the One You're With" peaked at #14 on Billboard's Hot 100.

The song has been recorded by many other artists, most notably by the Isley Brothers in 1971.

Suzanne

Suzanne struggled...badly. Who knows the hurt and emptiness that go into suicide? Well, for one — Suzanne.

She was a friend to a singer-songwriter who was going through a bunch of struggles himself. He'd been fighting a long battle with depression, substance abuse, and lack of direction. The loss of his band, The Flying Machine, didn't help, but now he was getting his shot...flying solo in England. He was going to record on the Beatles' Apple Records label, and he was seeing a little light in the tunnel. So, his friends didn't dare tell him about Suzanne's death.

He had been so fragile, they thought it might derail him and send him spiraling, so they waited six months and then broke the news. It hit hard. He understood her and her struggle.

The next day, he got up, took guitar in hand, put pen to paper and poured out his feelings on the page as he...

...James Taylor, started a song with the opening lyrics directed right at her: "Just yesterday morning they let me know you were gone...Suzanne the plans they made put an end to you".

The song "Fire and Rain" was born.

Side Notes:

Later, as a full-blown heroin addict, James checked into rehab. It was during that time that his desire to be free of the addiction and the loss of his band, "The Flying Machine", grew into the 3rd and 4th verses.

"Fire and Rain" was released as a single in 1970 and quickly rose to #3 on the Billboard Hot 100 chart - and launched his career.

It Was Worth the Wait

She opened up for him at the Troubadour in Hollywood, California on April 6, 1971. He was a big deal...she was becoming one. They immediately became members of the mutual admiration society.

Their show at the Troubadour received rave reviews, and when they flew back to New York, he asked her out. When the night came for their first date, she was nervous, he was late. She loved his music, along with a gazillion other fans, and probably wondered if the man behind such soulful lyrics would live up to the idea she had of him floating through her mind.

So...she waited, while those feelings grew inside, and when he finally got there, he sat with her on her bed. She grabbed her guitar, hitched a ride on an emotion, and wrote a song about exactly what she was feeling...

...right in front of him. It took about 15 minutes for Carly Simon to write "Anticipation" - all about waiting for her date...Cat Stevens.

We're all lucky he kept her waiting.

Side Notes:

"Anticipation" is the title track of her 2nd studio album released in 1971. It was a top hit in the U.S.

The night Carly opened for Cat Stevens, she met James Taylor backstage. She and James would later marry.

Louis
the Ranch Foreman

Louis was an older gentleman. He and his wife Clara were caretakers of a beautiful piece of land in the Santa Cruz mountains in Northern California. It was several hundred acres that had just been bought by a young singer-songwriter who'd been making a name for himself writing songs as honest and earthy as the property he was moving onto. He wrote about whatever and whoever was around him. He was also making some money for the first time in his life, enough to buy that property for $350,000.

It was 1970, the young singer was a loner, so it was a perfect place...and he felt safe there. He could be himself, and he was able to be that with Louis, and they connected. They talked a bunch about life and sometimes loneliness. Loneliness had often marked the young singer's life, and out of those conversations grew a lyric and a song about the things they had in common, despite their age difference.

The young singer said it straight-out in a song about, and really to, Louis. He said...

..."I'm a lot like you - I need someone to love me the whole day through". Louis Avila was the old man in the song "Old Man" on the huge 1972 album, "Harvest". The young singer-songwriter was Neil Young.

Side Notes:

"Old Man" was released as a single in 1972 and went to #31 on the Billboard chart.

James Taylor plays banjo on it - tuned like a guitar.

Neil Young named the ranch Broken Arrow and still lives there.

Danny's Damage

When the damage is done, it's done - you lose
your last shot. A bunch of great musicians
went out that way, and that was Danny's
deal. Danny Whitten was a singer-songwriter-
guitar player...a triple threat. But it was
another threat that got him and ruined all the
rest...heroin. He had so much promise, but he
couldn't shake his addiction.

Danny was playing guitar in Neil Young's band
Crazy Horse. When they were rehearsing to go
out on tour, Danny couldn't do it. He was so
out of it he could barely stay awake, let
alone hold a guitar. Neil and the band tried
to help, but in the end they had to fire
Danny. They bought him a plane ticket and
gave him $50 - only $50 because too much money
would have probably gone to the wrong places.

Neil had seen so many great artists go through
it, but this time it was in his own band. He
watched the daily devastation up close, and
it was personal...art being snuffed out by
a demon. Neil was filled with a bag full of
emotions and the most honest of them poured
into a song...

...a simple straight-forward reaction to seeing "The Needle and the Damage Done".

Shortly after arriving back home, Danny died of an overdose. Ironically, it was a lethal combo of Valium and alcohol that killed him that day, but heroin paved the road that got him there.

Side Notes:

"The Needle and the Damage Done" was recorded on the "Harvest" album in 1972.

No Parades

No parades...not usually. Not for the guys that came home from the war in Vietnam. They were showered more with questions than ticker tape, although there were a few exceptions.

Daniel was an exception. He was one of the lucky ones, or so everyone thought. His little hometown in Texas treated him like a hero. They knew the issues surrounding the war weren't his fault, so they cheered him. But...that was hard for him. He lived through it and was dying to put it behind him, but the attention wouldn't end. He had to know about the bitterness elsewhere...the comments, the questions and the overall reactions that greeted other returning soldiers. It was all over the news and was a very confusing time and a controversial war — controversial because of the reasons we were there, the way it was fought, and the way it ended. Folks were widely divided on the details of each side. He didn't want to dwell on it. He just wanted to go back to his simple life, but in the current climate, it didn't seem possible.

So, he decided his only chance was to get away for a while — way away. At the time, two songwriters had been following his story and wrote about it. So...

...in Bernie Taupin and Elton John's song inspired by a struggling solder, 'Daniel' boarded a plane and was 'headed to Spain', and they could see him 'waving goodbye'.

Side Notes:

The lyrics to "Daniel" were written by Bernie Taupin and the music by Elton John. That combo was responsible for many of Elton's big hits.

"Daniel" was on Elton's "Don't Shoot Me I'm Only the Piano Player" album.

It was released as a single in 1973 and went to #2 in the U.S. on the pop charts and #1 on the Adult Contemporary chart.

It went to #1 in Canada and the Top 5 in the UK.

Out of the Ashes
Rose a Song

It was the perfect place — a casino complex on the edge of a lake. It had the perfect sound to record an album and they rented a mobile studio to capture it. Everything was lined up, but they'd have to wait 'til the next night to record because that night another band was playing there...Frank Zappa and the Mothers of Invention. But then something happened that would change everybody's plans. Right in the middle of a guitar solo section during Zappa's song, "King Kong", some nut shot a flare gun into the ceiling and the whole place went up in flames. Well — the band waiting in the wings who wanted to record a live album was instead in the middle of what can only be called a happy accident...a serendipitous happening in the middle of craziness, despite the obvious horrifying event. It was like life handed them a stick with a marshmallow on it, since it was on fire anyway and something sweet came from it - a real musical gift.

The band planning to record the next night was Deep Purple. The casino was referred to as the 'gambling house' in the song born from this event. The location really *was* on the shoreline of Lake Geneva, in Montreux, Switzerland. They rented the mobile recording studio truck from the Rolling Stones, and all those visuals would soon give birth to a song that...

...Deep Purple would become most known for. Painting pictures with words, they just wrote what they saw..."Smoke on the water — fire in the sky".

Side Notes:

The writing was a band effort. "Smoke on the Water" was written by Ritchie Blackmore, Ian Gillian, Jon Lord, Roger Glover, and Ian Paice.

"Smoke on the Water" was recorded on their 1972 album "Machine Head".

It went to #4 on the Billboard charts in the summer of 1973.

Out of the Asylum

He was unwinding for the first time in a long
time. No easy feat for a high-powered music
executive and artist manager, one who seemed
to have the Midas touch. Every artist he was
working with was really taking off, and what
an amazing crop of talent, right when the
singer-songwriter genre was just coming to
light and shining down on everyone. He was a
workhorse, a mover and shaker with the phone
attached to his right hand about fifteen hours
a day. The downside of being great at what he
did was that everybody wanted something from
him. He was no different, and fed off the
energy. But sometimes folks don't realize how
much pressure they're under until they take
a break and get out from under it. Then they
find a weight being lifted, and that might
mean getting away...far away.

So that's what he and his good friend Joni
did. They went to Europe, and after awhile
it dawned on Joni that her friend David
was loosening up. She was seeing him in a
different light and she decided to document
it in song. There they were in one of the most
beautiful and inspiring cities in the world,
and it hit Joni Mitchell...

...that her friend David Geffen, who normally ran at full speed 24/7, chained to his work, looked to her that day like a "Free Man in Paris".

Side Notes:

"Free Man in Paris" appeared on Joni's 1974 album "Court and Spark". The album was released on the Asylum Records label which was founded and owned by David Geffen.

The song went to #22 on the Hot 100 chart and #2 on the Easy Listening chart.

It Was Mean...
But It Was Magic

It was a joke...a singer taking a little shot
at his brother, and it became the winning
piece of the song. It was just a great
straight rock song about getting love from
a bit of a wild woman. The simple lyric was
good, but that's not what really sold it.
The music was great, but that wasn't what
ultimately did it. The band was rockin' and
the singer was perfect for it. It was the
combo of all those things, and one more, which
propelled the song into greatness.

The singer took some liberties with the way
he sang the chorus lines on the first run
through. He did it as a joke toward his
brother and fully intended to sing it straight
after he played the joke version. But when he
did sing it straight, he didn't like it nearly
as much.

There was something about the sound of the
joking pieces that gave it its 'hookiness'.
Those pieces made it more memorable, so they
went back to it. The singer's name was Randy
Bachman of the band Bachman Turner Overdrive.
His brother, Gary, stuttered, so...

...when Randy sang the chorus to "You Ain't Seen Nothin' Yet", he sang "Ba ba ba ba baby you just ain't seen nu nu nu nu nothin' yet". It might have seemed a little mean, but it turned out to be the magic the song needed to put it over the top.

Side Notes:

"You Ain't Seen Nothin' Yet" was released in 1974, and in seven weeks went to the top of the Billboard Hot 100 chart. It was the only #1 single for BTO.

Randy Bachman had another #1 song when he was in The Guess Who and "American Woman" topped the charts.

Silly but Serious

Silly...at least that's how Bernie described it. Not the overall situation, just the scene — windows wide open and letting all the gas out. It seemed to him more of a frustrated cry for help than an actual suicide attempt. There was his friend, lying on the kitchen floor with a pillow under his head, and the windows wide open. You see, his friend had been battling depression over his upcoming marriage, a marriage that in truth shouldn't have been happening. He was about to walk down the aisle with the wrong person — wrong in so many ways. Bernie and his friend had that kind of relationship though, where they were brutally honest with each other in ways that no one understood but them.

Serious...Bernie's friend was still in a bad place but the gas was turned off. His friend got up and began working through it with the help of another friend named Long John Baldry, who encouraged him to call off the wedding, step back, and regroup. Bernie's friend was also his songwriting partner and the one who wrote the melodies and sang the songs they wrote. So as they got past it and back to work, Bernie got an idea for a song driven by his friend's struggle and half-hearted suicide attempt, and carved out a lyric from the viewpoint of his friend...

...Elton John. So, between Bernie Taupin's lyric, Elton's melody and voice, and Long John Baldry's help, when Elton John sang "Someone Saved My Life Tonight", it was true. Bernie wrote the lyric and Elton wrote the music just as they did with all their big hits.

Side Notes:

"Someone Saved My Life Tonight" was recorded on the album "Captain Fantastic and the Brown Dirt Cowboy".

It was the album's only single and was released in 1975.

It reached #4 on the Billboard Hot 100 chart.

Waitin' On a Plane

That's what they were doing...waiting to go to the airport. They were vacationing in Hawaii and were gonna head out in less than an hour — they being Leslie and her boyfriend who were staying with a friend there. Leslie's boyfriend was a singer-songwriter, a famous one, Graham Nash. It may have been raining outside, but the sun was shining inside in the form of serendipity. Rolling around in Graham's head was a bunch of bittersweet emotions that always came up when he went out on tour — excited to play, but leaving loved ones behind for an extended period of time. Those thoughts and emotions just needed something to poke them 'til they fell out like a piñata.

That poke came from a friend who was at the house where they were staying. He said, "You've got half an hour, why don't you just write a song before you go?" That was all Graham needed. He sat at the piano and took that suggestion as his opening line...

..."just a song before I go", and all those other thoughts about going out on the road filled up the rest. "Just a Song Before I Go" was written that day in 20 minutes.

Side Notes:

"Just a Song Before I Go" appeared on the 1977 album "Crosby, Stills & Nash".

It was released as a single in June of 1977 and went to #7 on the Billboard charts. It is CSN's biggest chart hit.

Before joining CSN, Graham was in the English band the Hollies, which took its name from their love of Buddy Holly.

Indian Poetry and a Woman's Intuition

It was just a simple guitar piece that he played to warm up his fingers. He didn't think much about it, but when his wife heard it, she did, and told him he should write some lyrics to it. He was the lead guitar player in a well-known rock band, but he was also known for his electric guitar. This piece was played on an acoustic guitar, so the idea of doing something more with it didn't occur to him. His wife thought it was beautiful and encouraged him to consider it, so he did. After all, if she loved it, it might hit a lot of other female fans the same way.

At the time, his career had been going really well. He had all the material things that success brings, but he was feeling a rising sense of angst about where all that fit into the big picture of life. He had been thinking a lot about big picture stuff when he came across a line in a poem...an American Indian poem. It seemed to sum up an emotion he was struggling to identify about the importance of things, material things, time spent and time wasted. The line in that poem did something else too. It felt like it would fit the vibe of that guitar piece his wife thought was so pretty. So, he decided to chase it and see if it connected — and sure enough, there was a marriage of a melody and a lyric idea, and a song was born. His name was...

...Kerry Livgren. His band was Kansas, and that line in the poem that connected to his thoughts and fit so well into that little finger warm-up was — "All we are is dust in the wind".

Side Notes:

Kerry thought the song was wrong for the band, but they wanted to record it.

It was released on their 1977 record "Point of Know Return".

The single was released in 1978 and went to #6 on the Billboard Hot 100 chart. It was the biggest hit Kansas would ever have.

Sources

Crosby, Stills & Nash – "Crosby, Stills & Nash: The Biography"

David Crosby – "Since Then"

Eric Clapton – "Clapton: The Autobiography"

"Fire and Rain: The Beatles, Simon & Garfunkel, James Taylor, CSNY, and the Lost Story of 1970"

"Girls Like Us: Carole King, Joni Mitchell, Carly Simon – and the Journey of a Generation"

Graham Nash – "Wild Tales"

"Laurel Canyon: The Inside Story of Rock-and-Roll's Legendary Neighborhood"

David Crosby – "The Autobiography of David Crosby - A Long Time Gone"

Neil Young – "Waging Heavy Peace"

Neil Young – "Shakey – The Autobiography of Neil Young"

"Tearing Down the Wall of Sound: The Rise and Fall of Phil Spector"

"The Rise and Rise of David Geffen"

"Waiting for the Sun: A Rock 'n' Roll History of Los Angeles"

Photo Credits

Cover photo: Aleksandra N / 123RF.com

Cover photo alteration & design: Cathy Arkle / cathyarkle.com

Back cover photo: Sergejs Rahunoks / 123RF.com

Back cover author photo: Noah Sellers

Page v: Fulya / Bigstock.com

Page vi, 28: Yuran-78 / Bigstock.com - Photo alteration: Cathy Arkle

Page x: Author photo: Sherie Sellers

Page xiii, 6, 12, 18: Illustration by Diddle / Bigstock.com

Page xiv: Jaycriss / Bigstock.com

Page 2: Redcouchphoto / Bigstock.com

Page 4: Carole King in the 1960s. Credit: Courtesy Concord Music Group

Page 16: Brickrena / Bigstock.com

Page 26: Richard Peterson / Bigstock.com

Page 27: Illustration Vector Design / Bigstock.com

Page 32: Warren Sellers

Page 44: AnnekaS / Bigstock.com

Page 46: Gordo25 / Bigstock.com

Page 52: Wikipedia Photographer: Benh LIEU SONG - Creative Commons Attribution-Share Alike 3.0 Unported license

Page 56: Publicity photo of Elton John from The Cher Show - Feb. 9, 1975

Page 58: Vladimir Veljanovski / Bigstock.com

Page 60: De Visu / Bigstock.com

At **Square Tree Publishing**, we believe your message matters. That is why our dedicated team of professionals is committed to bringing your literary texts and targeted curriculum to a global marketplace. We strive to make that message of the highest quality, while still maintaining your voice. We believe in you; therefore, we provide a platform through website design, blogs, and social media campaigns to showcase your unique message. Our innovative team offers a full range of services from editing to graphic design, inspired with an eye for excellence, so that your message is clearly and distinctly heard.

Whether you are a new writer needing guidance with each step of the process, or a seasoned writer, we will propel you to the next level of your development.

At **Square Tree Publishing**, it's all about **you**.

Take advantage of a free consultation.
Your opportunity is "Write Outside the Box"!

www.SquareTreePublishing.com

Made in the USA
San Bernardino, CA
05 October 2017